LUCY AND THE SATURDAY SURPRISE

by Melissa B. Kruger

illustrated by Samara Hardy

CROSSWAY

WHEATON, ILLINOIS

Lucy and the Saturday Surprise

Copyright © 2023 by Melissa B. Kruger

Illustrations © 2023 Crossway

Published by Crossway
1300 Crescent Street
Wheaton, Illinois 60187

Published in association with the literary agency of Wolgemuth & Associates, Inc.

Illustrations, book design, and cover design: Samara Hardy

First printing 2023

Printed in China

Scripture quotations are from the ESV® Bible (The Holy Bible, English Standard Version®), copyright © 2001 by Crossway, a publishing ministry of Good News Publishers. Used by permission. All rights reserved. The ESV text may not be quoted in any publication made available to the public by a Creative Commons license. The ESV may not be translated into any other language.

All emphases in Scripture quotations have been added by the author.

ISBN: 978-1-4335-8441-1

Library of Congress Cataloging-in-Publication Data

Names: Kruger, Melissa B., author. | Hardy, Samara, illustrator.
Title: Lucy and the Saturday surprise / Melissa B. Kruger ; illustrated by Samara Hardy.
Description: Wheaton, Illinois : Crossway, [2023] | Audience: Ages 3–7.
Identifiers: LCCN 2022030472 | ISBN 9781433584411 (hardcover)
Subjects: CYAC: Envy—Fiction. | Conduct of life—Fiction. | LCGFT: Picture books.
Classification: LCC PZ7.1.K7876 Lu 2023 | DDC [E]—dc23
LC record available at https://lccn.loc.gov/2022030472

Crossway is a publishing ministry of Good News Publishers.

RRDS			33	32	31	30	29	28	27	26	25	24	23
15	14	13	12	11	10	9	8	7	6	5	4	3	2	1

"Love is patient and kind; love does not envy. . . ."

1 CORINTHIANS 13:4

Lucy woke up with a jolt of excitement. It was Saturday—her favorite day of the week. She ran into her brother's room and jumped on his bed.

"Lewis, wake up!" she cried. "Let's go."

She ran down the stairs, with a half-awake Lewis following in her footsteps.

Dad greeted them both with a big smile and asked, "Are you ready to go?"

They jumped on their bikes and rode down the street to Sammy's, their favorite grocery store.

While Dad picked up a few items for his famous French toast, both Lewis and Lucy ran over to the candy carousel in the middle of the store. Dad looked over and smiled. "You can each pick one treat."

Lucy circled the carousel, thinking about which piece of candy she would choose. A purple sparkle pop? A giant pink gumball? A red licorice twist? She walked around and around, trying to choose. Finally, she decided: Sammy's Special Chocolate Square!

Lewis chose a lollipop with red and green and yellow and blue spiral swirls. They put all the groceries in the basket and headed home for breakfast.

After breakfast, they pulled out their candy. Lucy opened up her square. It had melted on the ride home! More chocolate ended up on her hands and face than in her mouth.

She looked at Lewis, slowly eating his lollipop. It looked so much better than the melted chocolate square. She should have picked the lollipop!

Lucy washed her hands and went outside to play. Lewis wrapped up his lollipop and went to join her on the swing.

When they came back inside, Lewis unwrapped his lollipop and sat at the table, enjoying his treat.

Again.

Lucy went in the other room and sat on the couch. She could hear him smacking his lips.

Slurp. Smack. Crunch.

The sounds got louder and louder.

It's not fair that he gets to keep eating his candy all day long. I wish I had a lollipop, she thought to herself. She covered her head with a pillow to drown out the sound.

Her dad came in the room and asked her to do a puzzle with him.

"I don't want to," she mumbled as she walked out of the room. All she could think about was the lollipop. She wished she hadn't picked the chocolate square.

As Lucy walked into the kitchen, Lewis wrapped up his lollipop and headed back outside to play.

"Do you want to come with me?" he asked.

"No," Lucy snapped, as she sat at the table. "I just played with you. You can play by yourself."

Lewis walked outside with a hurt look on his face, and Lucy was left alone with the lollipop.

The lollipop looked so good.

Lucy thought to herself, *I'll just move it to the counter so I don't have to look at it.*

She picked it up and could smell the sweet strawberry flavor.

The lollipop smelled so good.

She put it closer to her nose. She couldn't resist. She took a bite.

The lollipop tasted so good.

At that moment, Dad walked in the kitchen. "Why are you holding Lewis's lollipop?" he asked.

"Oh, I was just wrapping it up so it wouldn't get dirty!" Lucy said, hiding what she'd done. Dad looked at her with an eyebrow raised as she quickly put the lollipop on the counter and ran upstairs to her room.

She shut the door and crawled into her bed and pulled the covers up over her head. She felt terrible. The lollipop had tasted sweet to her tongue, but now she felt sick in her stomach.

She heard a knock at the door. "Can I come in?" asked Dad.

"Yes," Lucy mumbled from under the covers.

"Are you okay, Lucy? Is there anything you want to tell me?" She didn't want to tell her dad, but all at once the words started to gush out.

"I was sad that I picked the chocolate square and it was all mushy and melted by the time we got home. Lewis's lollipop looked so much better than my treat. I wanted to move it so that I wouldn't see it anymore, but then I smelled it, and I took a bite. I thought it was going to make me feel better to have a bite of the lollipop, but I feel miserable."

Her dad sat gently on the bed. "Lucy, when we feel grumpy because someone has something we want, it's called *envy*. It follows a pattern: You *saw* something you wanted, then you *coveted* it, then you *took* a lick from your brother, and then you tried to *hide* what you'd done."

Lucy wiped away her tears and looked up at her dad with an inquisitive gaze. "You said it follows a pattern. Do you mean other people have envy too?"

"Yes. The Bible tells of many people who wanted things that didn't belong to them, and their envy led them to make bad choices. A man named Achan in the book of Joshua saw some gold and silver, coveted it, took it, and tried to hide from God what he had done.

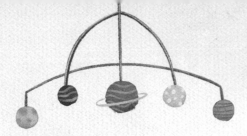

"We can't really hide our coveting. Eventually, our envy causes us to act unkindly or take something that isn't ours."

"I feel bad about eating Lewis's lollipop. What can I do?" Lucy asked.

"Well, I'm glad you told me the truth and stopped trying to hide. When you feel envy toward someone, it's best to confess what you are feeling to someone you trust. But I think you also need to confess to Lewis what you did."

Lucy and Dad walked downstairs and found Lewis sitting in the den working on a puzzle with Mom. Lucy felt like she had knots in her stomach. She didn't want to tell him.

She finally blurted out, "Lewis, I'm sorry. I did something bad.
I wanted the treat you picked today, and I took a bite of your lollipop."

Lewis looked at her with a surprised look on his face. "That's okay!" he replied. "Is that what you were so grumpy about all morning? I would have given you a bite if you had just asked me."

Lucy felt so relieved. "I'm sorry for being grumpy. I'd love to play with you. Can I help you with the puzzle?"

"Sure! I just found a corner piece," Lewis said.

"It goes right here," Lucy replied, with a smile on her face. She felt better than she had all day.

THE END

Note to Grown-Ups

FOR LUCY, SATURDAY'S BIGGEST SURPRISE wasn't about the treat at all—it was realizing that sometimes getting what you want isn't what really makes you happy.

Everyone has desires. We long for good things: food, clothing, friends, and family. However, when our desires turn covetous, we either want a good thing in a wrong way or we want something that God forbids.

God had expressly prohibited the fruit from the tree of the knowledge of good and evil, and that's why Eve's desire for it was wrong (Gen. 2:17). When Achan coveted the spoils from the battle at Jericho, he disobeyed God's command (Josh. 6:18–19). In both instances, their covetous desires followed a similar pattern: *see, covet, take,* and *hide*. As Achan recounted:

> Truly I have sinned against the LORD God of Israel, and this is what I did: when I *saw* among the spoil a beautiful cloak from Shinar, and 200 shekels of silver, and a bar of gold weighing 50 shekels, then I *coveted* them and *took* them. And see, they are *hidden* in the earth inside my tent, with the silver underneath. (Josh. 7:20–21)

As we talk about envy with our children, it's helpful to explain that our sinful desires don't simply stay inside our hearts. Eventually, wrong desires bear bad fruit, and they will lead us to take from others in harmful ways (James 1:14–15).

Looking over the fence and wanting what someone has will only make children (and adults) less happy. As Proverbs 14:30 teaches, "A tranquil heart gives life to the flesh, but envy makes the bones rot." Help children discover that contentment—being thankful for what you have—is the alternative to envy, and it leads to greater joy. We can grow in this area by thanking the Lord regularly for all that we have and rejoicing in his goodness (1 Thess. 5:16–18)!

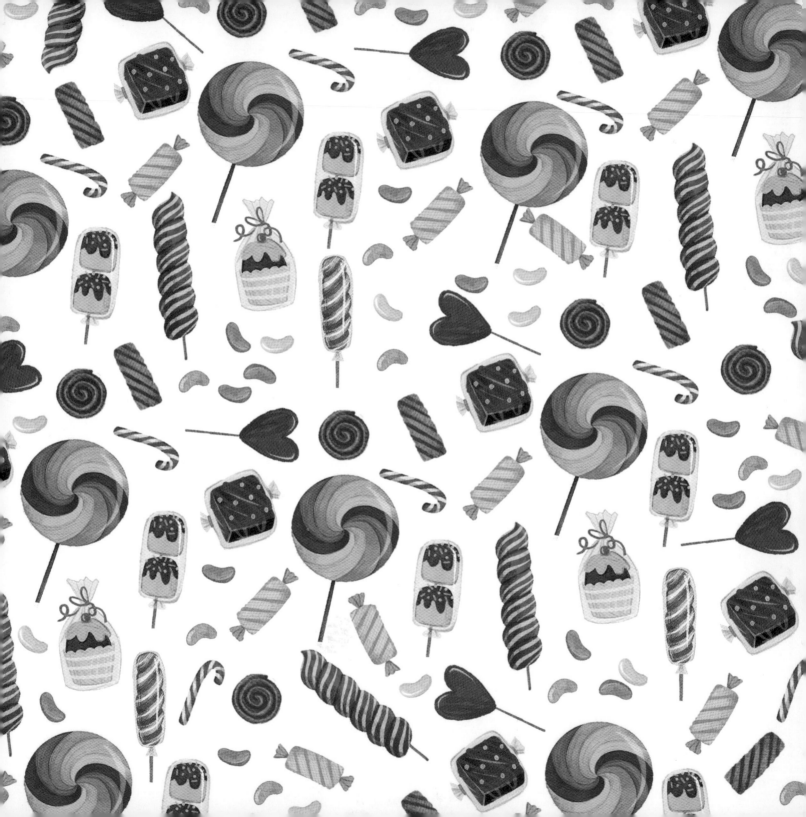